SUPER SMART INFORMATION STRATEGIES

SOCIAL STUDIES PROJECTS THAT SHINE

by Sara Wilkie

CHERRY LAKE PUBLISHING • ANN ARBOR, MICHIGAN

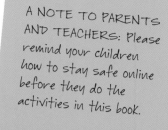

A NOTE TO PARENTS AND TEACHERS: Please remind your children how to stay safe online before they do the activities in this book.

CHERRY LAKE Publishing

A NOTE TO KIDS: Always remember your safety comes first!

Published in the United States of America
by Cherry Lake Publishing
Ann Arbor, Michigan
www.cherrylakepublishing.com

Content Adviser: Gail Dickinson, PhD,
Associate Professor, Old Dominion University,
Norfolk, Virginia

Book design and illustration: The Design Lab

Photo credits: Page 4, ©Dawn Shearer-Simonetti/Shutterstock, Inc.; page 5, ©Dmitriy Shironosov/Shutterstock, Inc.; page 6, ©archana bhartia/Shutterstock, Inc.; page 10, ©Isaiahlove/Dreamstime.com; page 18, iStockphoto.com/myshotz; page 20, ©Patrickwang/Dreamstime.com; page 23, ©Monkey Business Images/Shutterstock, Inc.; page 27, © Zurijeta/Shutterstock, Inc.

Library of Congress Cataloging-in-Publication Data
Wilkie, Sara.
  Super smart information strategies: social studies projects that shine/ by Sara Wilkie.
       p. cm.—(Information explorer)
  Includes bibliographical references and index.
  ISBN-13: 978-1-61080-123-2 (lib. bdg.)
  ISBN-13: 978-1-61080-269-7 (pbk.)
  1. Social sciences—Study and teaching (Elementary)—Activity programs—Juvenile literature. 2. Project method in teaching—Juvenile literature. I. Title.
  LB1584.W489 2012
  371.3'6—dc22   2011016113

Cherry Lake Publishing would like to acknowledge
the work of The Partnership for 21st Century Skills.
Please visit www.21stcenturyskills.org for more information.

Printed in the United States of America
Corporate Graphics Inc.
July 2011
CLFA09

Table of Contents

CHAPTER ONE
Organizing Your Team

Team members must collaborate to make a successful project.

Have you ever worked as a member of a team to get something done? If you have, you know how important it is for everyone to work together. Teamwork means agreeing on a goal and working together to reach that goal.

Collaborating on a social studies project requires teamwork. In the pages ahead, you will work as a member of a team to pick a social studies topic. Your team will dig to discover more and then work together to share what you've learned with others.

Social studies deals with the study of people, groups, societies, and cultures. There are a lot of topics in social studies. Your team may be able to pick any topic to work on, but sometimes you are assigned a topic. Social studies fairs are like science fairs. But instead of experiments, teams showcase their research or problem-solving skills in social studies. Some fairs have a list of topics from which your team must choose. Other fairs do not. Knowing the rules and goals for your project will give your team a place to start.

First, your group will need to agree on a topic or event. Members should consider their own interests and think about events that catch their attention. Your

Maybe there is a certain country or region your team can learn more about.

Reading through a newspaper can give you
ideas for project topics.

team will be more motivated if a project is chosen that
interests all of you. Try listening to current news sto-
ries. Magazines, newspapers, television, and online
news sources can offer ideas to get you started, too.
Some Web sites offer lists of project ideas. You can also
tour social studies fairs to see what topics other stu-
dents are exploring. You don't want to copy someone
else's work, but sometimes seeing another project can
help spark ideas for your own.

When your team comes up with a list of ideas for
a topic, you'll want to discuss them. Listen carefully
to each other's comments and suggestions. This can be
hard, especially if you have a topic you really like. But
when you are working with a team, it is important to
consider everyone's ideas before making a decision.

After a topic has been selected, the team needs to work together to narrow the focus and identify a driving question. This is the one big question that the team decides to pose about the topic. The driving question will clearly define the focus of the project. It is important for everyone on your team to agree on the driving question. Brainstorming is one effective way of thinking about all of the possible questions your team could pick. In a brainstorm, you jot down questions that people come up with in a short amount of time. As you do this, keep in mind the rules and goals for your project. When the time is up, the team can discuss the possibilities and select a question for the project.

TRY THIS!

Make sure each group member has
an index card and a pen or pencil.
Spread out so you have enough room
to work independently. Think about
your group's chosen topic:
- What about this topic interests
  you the most?
- What questions do you have
  about the person or event?

What about this topic interests you the most?

What questions do you have about the person or event?

Write down your answers. Then regroup as a team. Listen to each other's questions, but do not comment on them. There will be time to discuss them in the next step. Be sure each member of your group has a chance to share. Listen respectfully and carefully:

- Do any ideas or questions sound similar to yours?
- Are there parts of others' questions that fit with parts of yours?
- Are there other questions that catch your attention?

Finally, discuss each question as a team:

- How well does the question relate to your topic?
- Will it capture viewers' attention?
- Is it broad enough?
- Is there a way your team can blend parts of different questions to come up with a stronger one?

Do your best to decide on a driving question that each member is interested in investigating. Reaching a consensus will pay off in the end!

Is there a way to blend different ideas to come up with a stronger idea?

CHAPTER TWO
Creating a Place to Work Together

You can work with other team members to create a digital space for your project.

Keeping track of information and resources gathered is important in social studies. Setting up a digital work-space is one way to help your team stay organized and focused. It will also allow members to work in different places and at different times. A digital space, such as a blog or a wiki, lets group members share resources, Web sites, and notes. You can post audio, video, text, or picture files. You can even invite experts on your topic to contribute to your notes or offer feedback on your work.

Any time you work online, it's important to remember some basic guidelines. This SMART strategy will help you work safely and responsibly on the Internet:

Safety—Personal information should never be shared on the Internet. Always ask an adult if the information you are posting is appropriate to share. Report any inappropriate content to an adult right away.

Manners—Be respectful of others and their opinions. Always use polite language. Remember to give credit to the original author when sharing someone else's work.

Adult Supervision—Always ask a parent, teacher, or other trusted adult for permission before working on the Internet.

Responsibility—You are responsible for everything you post. No exceptions! Be sure your information is accurate, relevant, and reliable.

Teamwork—Follow through on your roles and responsibilities. Support and encourage your teammates. Add value to their work by giving detailed and specific feedback. Be sure to word your thoughts in positive ways.

There are many options for collaborating online. For

our example, we will use a wiki. A wiki is a collection
of Web pages that allow users to edit, change, and add
information. Ask an adult for help setting up a wiki
space that your group can use for this project.

TRY THIS!

Now that you have a topic and a driving
question, it is important to consider what your
team understands about it before beginning
your investigation. To get started, your team
can follow these steps:
1. Create a new page on a wiki site (the specific
   steps to do this may be slightly different,
   depending on which site you choose).
2. Title your page with the name of your topic.
3. Click the Edit button.

4. Add the headings listed below:
   Our Topic
   Our Driving Question
   We Understand
   We Wonder
   Our Strategies
   Our Resources

continued ⟶

What major question drives your team's project?

5. Post your topic and driving question below those headings.
6. Post what you understand about your topic under We Understand.
7. Post what you wonder, or what questions you have about your topic, under We Wonder.
8. Post your strategies for finding answers to your questions, working as a team, or staying on task under Our Strategies.
9. As research is done, add links and other citations under the Our Resources heading.

It will help to give each member of your team a specific job with the wiki. Even so, everyone will be responsible for taking care of the page.

Discusstion Starter

TRY THIS!

Discuss the following roles and decide which member of the team will be responsible for each role. Decide as a group how often each person will do his or her job.

DISCUSSION STARTER

A Discussion Starter uses the discussion tab on your group's wiki page to ask questions about what the group is producing and how the work is going. This person asks what parts of the work are challenging members and what parts are complete. A Discussion Starter also helps the group set due dates and complete required tasks.

continued ⟶

Link Layer

LINK LAYER

Links are important because they show where you found your information. They give readers a place to look if they want to learn more. The Link Layer is responsible for checking the links to be sure they are:
- Accurate
- Working
- Placed in the right spot on the wiki page

WIKI WEEDER

It's important for your group's wiki to look organized and reliable. Readers will wonder about the accuracy of your information if they see spelling errors. They might not bother to read information that is too hard to understand or follow.

The Wiki Weeder is responsible for weeding out and correcting the following kinds of problems on your wiki page:

- Inaccurate information
- Irrelevant information
- Inappropriate information
- Misspelled words
- Mislabeled headings, images, videos, etc.

Wiki Weeder

FACT DIGGER

You want to be sure that you have posted enough information to help others understand what you're learning. The Fact Digger is responsible for checking the information and facts posted on the wiki page.

- Are the facts clear and easy to understand?
- Do they help answer the driving or guiding questions?
- Is there enough information?
- Is the information organized in a way that makes it easy to follow?

Fact Digger

The guiding questions of most social studies projects
begin with Who, What, When, Where, Why, and How.
At the top of your wiki page, add the heading *Guiding
Questions*. Under this heading, add each of the
following sections:

1. Who is involved?
2. What happened?
3. Where did this happen?
4. Where else are the
   effects of this event felt?
5. When did this event
   begin/end?
6. Why did this happen?
7. Why is this considered an
   important event?
8. How has this event
   shaped the world we live
   in today?

You will need to do
some initial research to find
answers to these questions.
Check several sources to
see where you can get the
best information for your topic. Sources can include
your school or local library and the Internet. You can
talk to people from your community or experts in the
field. You may also be able to speak to people living in

the area where the event took place, or to other people with connections to your topic. The more sources you find, the stronger your information will be.

As you gather information, it is important to use your critical thinking skills. Check to be sure that each source is reliable and that the information is accurate and relevant. Then add your notes to the *Guiding Questions* section on your wiki page.

You may need to do some digging to make sure you have reliable sources.

TRY THIS!

Before posting any information on your team page, work through this checklist:
1. Is the information reliable and accurate? How do I know?
2. Is the author an expert? How can I tell?
3. Does this Web site have a reliable organization or expert behind it?
4. Can I tell where the author of this site found this information?
5. If not, can I find this information in at least two other reliable places?

CHAPTER THREE
Seeing All Sides

⌐ Everyone has his or her own perspective.

Have you ever had a hard time agreeing with a brother or sister? How about with a friend? Agreeing with another person can be hard when you don't share the same point of view, or perspective. Thinking about a situation from the perspective of everyone involved is important.

Because social studies deals with people and events, perspectives are particularly important to your team's project. Look for answers to your guiding questions from the different points of view of your topic's stakeholders. Stakeholders are people who are important to a society or event, or who have a lot to lose or gain in an issue. Your team's stakeholders are the people listed on your team's wiki under "Who is involved?" As a team, decide who will research and document each perspective. If there are more stakeholders than the number of people in your group, decide which perspectives are most important or would be the most interesting to learn about.

As you investigate a particular stakeholder, remember that people in different groups have different goals. Stakeholders involved in the same event often have different goals, too. Be careful not to depend on just one person's understanding of the event. Consider the situation for yourself and draw your own conclusions.

At the top of your wiki page, add a heading for each stakeholder. Under each heading, record the name of the teammate who will gather information from the perspective of that stakeholder. Post notes and related resources on your wiki page, under your stakeholder's name.

Consider This

As you research a particular perspective, it often helps to pose questions with the important starting words we've discussed:

- WHO are the stakeholders?
- WHAT is the issue?
- WHAT information about this group is important for others to know?
- WHAT is this stakeholder doing to solve the issue?
- HOW are the different stakeholders connected to each other?
- WHEN did this issue first begin?
- WHERE does this stakeholder work? Live?
- WHERE does this issue take place?
- WHY does this stakeholder group feel the way it does about this issue?
- WHY does this issue matter to this stakeholder?

CHAPTER FOUR
Digging to Discover

Watching an interview can help you learn a person's perspective on a situation.

It is important to look at primary sources when investigating your stakeholders. Primary sources are authentic artifacts of history. These include original documents, interviews, and images of objects that were created during the time you are investigating. Primary sources can be found at your local library or online at Web sites such as the Library of Congress. Asking a librarian for help can lead you to interesting sources. Primary sources can be strong links to the different perspectives of your topic.

Secondary sources present another understanding or interpretation of primary sources. These are published by someone who wasn't present at or directly involved with an event.

As you investigate a particular issue, keep in mind who is involved and why. Listen to speeches and interviews, and look at artifacts. Combine several primary sources to gain a better understanding of an issue. Researchers use triangulation to verify facts, which means they make sure at least three reliable sources agree on a fact.

The following questions will help you understand the information you find:
- Is this a primary or secondary source?
- Who created this source? When?
- What powerful words and ideas about my topic are expressed?
- What feelings and thoughts does the information trigger in me?
- What questions does it raise?
- What biases or stereotypes do I see?
- Are there other primary or secondary sources that support or contradict this information?
- If it's a primary source:
  - What was happening during the time it was created?
  - Why did someone think it was important to create this?
  - Who was their audience?
  - What were they hoping to accomplish?

Using research techniques from your media specialist or teacher, dig up answers to your remaining questions. Use a combination of primary and secondary sources. Look for interesting facts and details that support your topic and help others understand your perspective. Add you answers to your wiki. Include video, audio, links, images, and other resources that support what you learn.

Research Checklist

As you gather information and post it on your group wiki, work through this checklist:

☐ I have collected important information that relates to the Who, What, Where, When, Why, and How questions.

☐ I have explained the information in ways that address all sides of these questions.

☐ My notes are grouped according to the questions they help to answer.

☐ I have posted notes using my own words.

☐ I used my own words to clearly summarize my research.

☐ I have found quality Web sites with information on the perspective I am researching.

☐ I have used a variety of resources.

☐ I have triangulated the information I am using.

☐ I have properly cited each of my sources.

☐ I can explain why I included each source.

The Internet can help you connect with people around the world.

Anyone with an Internet connection can see the work you're doing on the wiki. This means they can work with you, too. You can invite others from around the world to collaborate with you on your wiki page for any project. Think about how powerful it would be to work with and learn from someone who was actually involved in the event you're researching! What could they share to help you better understand the situation? Connecting with people who have firsthand knowledge of the event will make your work more accurate. Remember, though, to ask an adult before trying to connect with someone who is involved in, or remembers being a part of, your topic.

CHAPTER FIVE

Drawing Conclusions and Putting It All Together

Have the Link Layer, Wiki Weeder, and Fact Digger do one final check of your wiki page. Review the information that has been posted. Carefully consider the perspectives offered by your teammates. Consider how each of these groups and their perspectives connect to your project's driving question. What have you learned through your research that will help your team answer your driving question? What questions still remain?

Have the Discussion Starter add the following topics to your discussion tab:

ANSWERS—What is your answer to our driving question? Use information from your research and our wiki page to back up your answer.

QUESTIONS—What questions do you still have? Have team members respond to each question.

As a team, share and discuss the answers posted for the driving question.

- Which answers most directly respond to the driving question?
- Are there elements from each that can be blended to create a stronger response?
- Are there artifacts or primary sources that can be included to strengthen the team's answer?
- As a team, share and discuss the questions that still remain.
- Do any of the remaining questions need to be answered in order to address the driving question?

You've researched your event, considered the different perspectives involved, and come to an agreement on the answer(s) to your driving question. Now it is time to share your understanding with the world! There are many ways your team can present what you've learned. First, check what the rules are for presentations at your social studies fair.

Creating a presentation that grabs your viewer's attention is important. You can present information in a way that highlights the people, time period, or events involved. For example, you could present a news report or student summit where your team responds to the driving question from the stakeholders' perspectives. A digital storybook that includes primary sources might be interesting, too. No matter how your team decides to share what's been learned, be sure to work together to create something interesting and strong!

Checklist

Work through the following checklist with your group as you collaborate to create your presentation.

☐ We cite a significant amount of evidence to answer the Who, What, Where, When, Why, and How of our driving question.

☐ Our information is easy to understand, accurate, and relevant.

☐ We include both primary and secondary sources of information.

☐ We introduce, explain, and connect the concerns of each stakeholder group to our driving question.

☐ If possible, we identify the outcome of the event.

☐ Our presentation meets all additional requirements for our project as outlined by our teacher or the organizer of the social studies fair.

CHAPTER SIX
Reflecting on Teamwork

With the presentation finished, you can reflect on how things went.

To grow as a learner, it helps to dig through your experiences. You worked hard to be sure that the information you included was relevant and accurate. You also worked as an important member of a team. You divided the roles and responsibilities of your group, and you worked together to design and create your social studies project. You relied on one another to get the job done.

TRY THIS!

Peer feedback is an important part of learning and growing as a team. The discussion tab at the top of your wiki page is a great place to post feedback. Have the Discussion Starter add a new topic for each member of the team, using the member's first name as the title. Then think about the teamwork of each member.

- How equally did that team member share in the workload?
- In what ways did he or she listen to, encourage, or ask questions of others in order to help the team?
- How well did each team member follow through on his or her wiki role?

Post meaningful feedback and suggestions for each member. Use descriptive words, so your reader can clearly understand your comments. Word your thoughts in positive ways. Be polite! When you're done, check to see what feedback your peers offered on your work.

It's not always fun to read peer feedback. Sometimes people suggest changes or disagree with your work. But remember that hearing what others have to say can help you learn about yourself and how you can improve your work. As you explore different perspectives of a an issue, you will come to realize that there are many sides to every situation. Challenge yourself to consider multiple points of view in every situation. What you learn might surprise you!

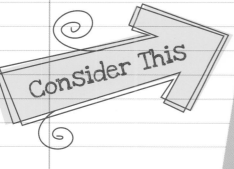

Consider This

- What feedback did your peer(s) offer?
- How might it help to improve your work?
- What suggestions do you agree with?
- How might they strengthen your teamwork skills?
- What suggestions do you disagree with? Consider them from your teammate's perspective. What questions could you ask to better understand what he or she was thinking?

Glossary

biases (BYE-uhs-ehz) personal judgments or prejudices

blog (BLAWG) a Web site that has a personal, online journal with entries from its author or authors

citations (sy-TAY-shunz) specific references

collaborating (kuh-LAB-uh-ray-teeng) working together to do something

consensus (kuhn-SEN-suhss) an agreement among all people in a discussion or meeting

guiding questions (GIDE-ing KWES-chenz) questions to guide or lead research and discussions

inappropriate (in-uh-PROH-pree-ut) not right or proper for the situation, time, or place

perspective (per-SPEK-tiv) a point of view or outlook

stakeholders (STAYK-hol-derz) people or groups who share an interest in a topic or issue

stereotypes (STER-ee-oh-tipes) an overly simple idea or opinion about a person, group, or thing that is shared by many people

summit (SUM-it) a conference or meeting of high-level leaders, usually called to shape a program of action

triangulated (trye-ANG-gyuh-lay-ted) found three resources or sets of data with the same information to help verify facts and ideas

wiki (WI-kee) a Web site that allows users to add and edit content and information

Find Out More

BOOKS

Cornwall, Phyllis. *Super Smart Information Strategies: Put It All Together*. Ann Arbor, MI: Cherry Lake Publishing, 2010.

Pascaretti, Vicki, and Sara Wilkie. *Super Smart Information Strategies: Team Up Online*. Ann Arbor, MI: Cherry Lake Publishing, 2010.

Pike, Kathy, Jean Mumper, and Paula Krieg. *25 Totally Terrific Social Studies Activities*. New York: Scholastic, 2009

WEB SITES

The Library of Congress

www.loc.gov/index.html

Explore this site to discover many primary source documents and artifacts.

National History Day

www.ushistory.org/nhdphilly/index.htm

Learn more about how you can participate in the National History Day competition.

Index

About the Author

Sara Wilkie is a learner, teacher, and teacher coach. She enjoys blending and test-driving ideas, and is incredibly fortunate to engage and learn with some of the thinkers who inspire her most! Sara is especially motivated by the support & encouragement of her home team!